FAVORITE
BASEBALL
★ TEAMS ★

PHILADELPHIA
PHILLIES

BY K. C. KELLEY

The Child's World®

Published by The Child's World®
1980 Lookout Drive • Mankato, MN 56003-1705
800-599-READ • www.childsworld.com

ACKNOWLEDGMENTS
The Child's World®: Mary Berendes,
    Publishing Director
The Design Lab: Kathleen Petelinsek, Design
Shoreline Publishing Group, LLC: James
    Buckley Jr., Production Director

PHOTOS
Cover: Focus on Baseball
Interior: All photos by Focus on Baseball except:
AP/Wide World: 9, 10, 17, 18, 22 (main), 26 (inset);
Getty Images: 22 (inset)

LIBRARY OF CONGRESS
CATALOGING-IN-PUBLICATION DATA
Kelley, K. C.
    Philadelphia Phillies / by K.C. Kelley.
        p. cm. — (Favorite baseball teams)
    Includes index.
    ISBN 978-1-60253-381-3 (library bound : alk. paper)
    1. Philadelphia Phillies (Baseball team)—History—
Juvenile literature. I. Title. II. Series.
    GV875.P45K45 2010
    796.357'640974811--dc22   2009039452

Printed in the United States of America
Mankato, Minnesota
November 2009
F11460

On the cover:
Ryan Howard, First Base

CONTENTS

Go, Phillies!

Philadelphia is called the "City of Brotherly Love." It's also the City of Baseball Love! Phillies fans are some of the most loyal—and loudest—in baseball. They haven't had a lot of winning teams to watch over the years. In recent seasons, though, the Phillies have been one of baseball's best. And the fans certainly love that! Let's meet the Phillies.

Big stretch by a big guy! Phillies first baseman Ryan Howard reaches ▶ out to make the catch!

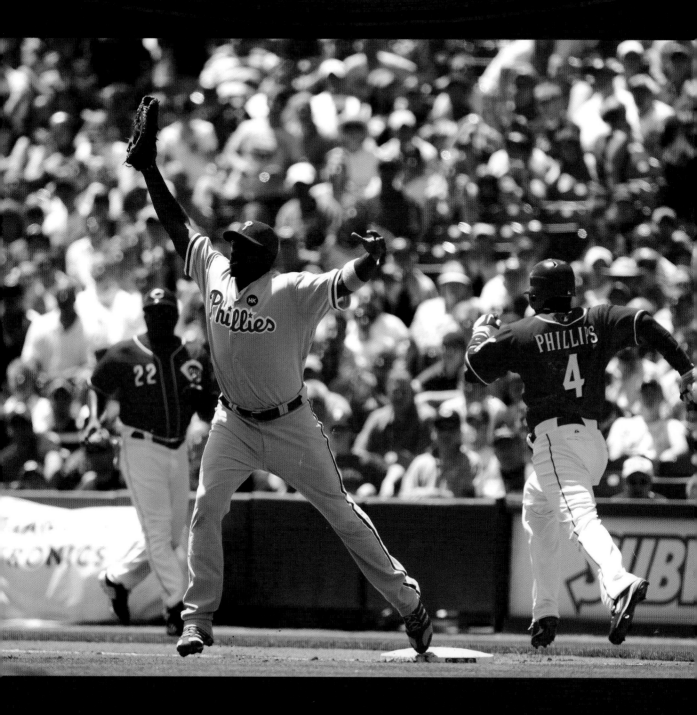

Who Are the Phillies?

The Philadelphia Phillies are a team in baseball's National League (N.L.). The N.L. joins with the American League to form Major League Baseball. The Phillies play in the East Division of the N.L. The division winners get to play in the league playoffs. The playoff winners from the two leagues face off in the **World Series**. The Phillies have won two World Series championships.

◀ A close play at second! Phillies **shortstop** Jimmy Rollins gathers in the throw from the catcher.

7

Where They Came From

The Philadelphia Phillies have been around for a long time. In fact, they joined the National League in 1883! They became the Phillies in 1890 and haven't changed their name since. No other Major League team has played that long with the same name and in the same city. In their first 67 years, they finished first once and second five times. In many other years, they were near the bottom of the N.L.

Outfielder Dick Sisler and **manager** Eddie Sawyer were happy after this ▶ World Series game win in 1950, but they lost the Series to the Yankees.

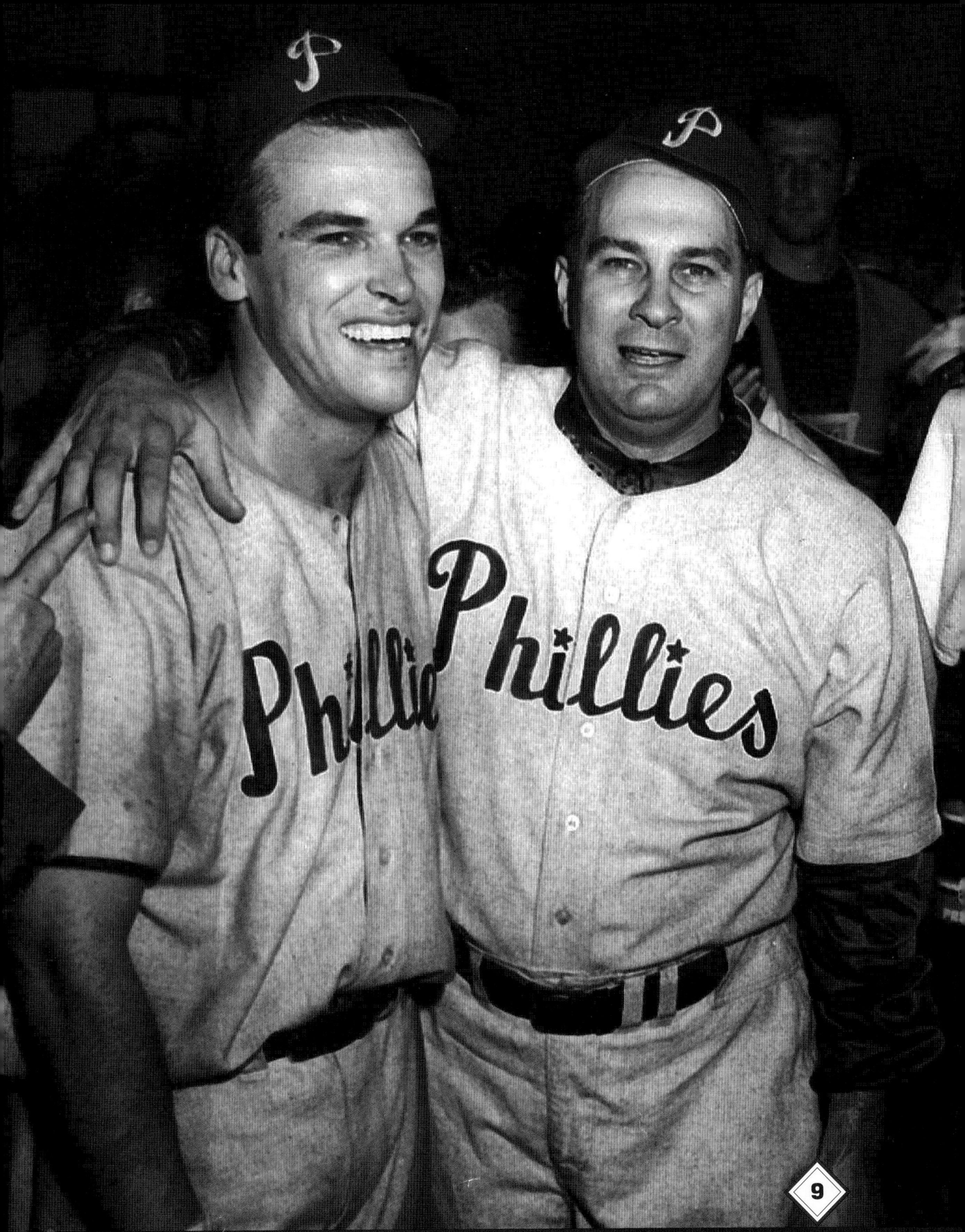
Phillies
Phillies

Who They Play

The Philadelphia Phillies play 162 games each season. That includes 18 games against the other teams in their division, the N.L. East. The Phillies have won eight N.L. East championships. The other East teams are the Atlanta Braves, the Florida Marlins, the New York Mets, and the Washington Nationals. Philadelphia's games against the Mets are always exciting! The Phillies also play some teams from the American League. Their A.L. **opponents** change every year.

◄ The Phillies' Jimmy Rollins sends a New York Mets player flying with this hard slide!

Where They Play

Since 2004, the Phillies have played in Citizens Bank Park. Fans like it much more than their old home in Veterans Stadium. Citizens Bank has real grass, for one thing. And it was made just for baseball. At Veterans, the team shared the field with the Eagles football team. Outside the ballpark, fans can visit statues of Phillies all-time stars: Richie Ashburn, Robin Roberts, Steve Carlton, and Mike Schmidt.

Phillies fans fill the seats of Citizens Bank Park to cheer for their team. ▶

13

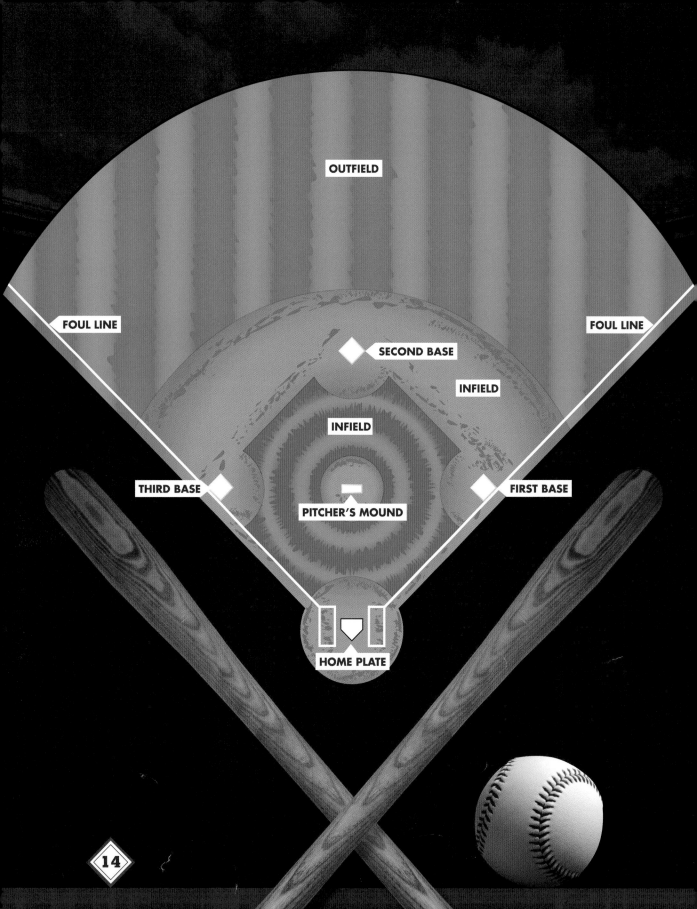

OUTFIELD

FOUL LINE

FOUL LINE

SECOND BASE

INFIELD

INFIELD

THIRD BASE

FIRST BASE

PITCHER'S MOUND

HOME PLATE

The Baseball Diamond

Baseball games are played on a diamond. Four bases form this diamond shape. The bases are 90 feet (27 m) apart. The area around the bases is called the **infield**. At the center of the infield is the pitcher's mound. The grass area beyond the bases is called the **outfield**. White lines start at **home plate** and go toward the outfield. These are the foul lines. Baseballs hit outside these lines are out of play. The outfield walls are about 300–450 feet (91–137 m) from home plate.

Big Days!

The Phillies have had some great seasons in their history. Here are three of the best:

1915: After 32 years, the Phillies finally won a league championship. They lost in the World Series to the Boston Red Sox. The Sox were led by a pitcher named Babe Ruth.

1980: Finally! After nearly one-hundred years in the N.L., the Phillies won their first World Series.

2008: This year's Phillies had slugging power and great pitching. They beat the Tampa Bay Rays in five games to win their second World Series.

Brad Lidge is ready to celebrate with catcher Raul Castro after the Phillies' ▶ big win in 2008.

Tough Days!

Not every season can end with a World Series win. Here are some of the toughest seasons in Phillies history:

1923: The Phillies have had some bad stretches. This was one of the worst. They finished at the bottom of the N.L. It was their fourth last-place finish in five years!

1964: The Phillies led the N.L. by 6 ½ games on September 18. Less than two weeks later, they had lost the lead— and their chance at the World Series. The season was known as the "Philly Flop."

1973: The Phillies finished in last place in the division . . . for the third season in a row!

◀ Manager Gene Mauch (pointing) could only sit and watch sadly as his team faded in 1964.

Meet the Fans

Phillies fans are famous for their booing! They can be tough on teams that don't do well, but they love teams that win! The fans went crazy in 2008 when their team won baseball's biggest prize. They greeted their World Series champs with a huge parade through downtown. The biggest Phillies fan of all is a giant, green . . . thing! Since 1978, the Phillie Phanatic has been one of baseball's most famous **mascots**.

The Phillie Phanatic is a fan favorite. He sometimes rides around the park on ▸ this little motor cart.

Steve Carlton, pitcher

Heroes Then . . .

Chuck Klein was a star slugger for the Phillies in the 1930s. He won the **Triple Crown** in 1933. In the 1950s, pitcher Robin Roberts was one of baseball's best. In the 1960s, slugger Dick Allen was one of the top home-run threats. The best Phillies player of all time was Mike Schmidt. This **Hall of Fame** third baseman hit 548 home runs from 1972 to 1989. He also won 10 **Gold Gloves** for **defense**. Phillies pitcher Steve Carlton won four **Cy Young Awards**. In 1972, he won 27 games. All the other Phillies pitchers together only won 32!

◀ Mike Schmidt is probably the best all-around third baseman ever.
Inset: Steve Carlton was a great pitcher on bad teams!

Heroes Now . . .

The Phillies have a trio of great players that helped them win the 2008 World Series. Slugging first baseman Ryan Howard was the N.L. **Most Valuable Player** (MVP) in 2006. He reached 200 homers in his career faster than any player in baseball history! Shortstop Jimmy Rollins was the 2007 N.L. MVP. He's a great team leader and a terrific base stealer. Second baseman Chase Utley is a four-time **All-Star**. He has lots of power for a second baseman. Lefty Cole Hamels is the pitching ace. He was the MVP of the team's 2008 World Series win.

Cole Hamels, Pitcher

Jimmy Rollins, Shortstop

Ryan Howard, First Base

BATTING HELMET

BAT

BATTING GLOVE

CATCHER'S MASK

CATCHER'S MITT

CHEST PROTECTOR

TEAM PANTS

CATCHER'S SHIN GUARD

BASEBALL CLEATS

Raul Castro, Catcher

Gearing Up

Baseball players all wear a team jersey and pants. They have to wear a team hat in the field and a helmet when batting. Take a look at Jayson Werth and Raul Castro to see some other parts of a baseball player's uniform.

THE BASEBALL

A Major League baseball weighs about 5 ounces (142 g). It is 9 inches (23 cm) around. A leather cover surrounds hundreds of feet of string. That string is wound around a small center of rubber and cork.

SPORTS STATS

Here are some all-time career records for the Philadelphia Phillies. All the stats are through the 2009 season.

HOME RUNS

Mike Schmidt, 548
Del Ennis, 259

RUNS BATTED IN

Mike Schmidt, 1,595
Del Ennis, 1,124

BATTING AVERAGE

Nap Lajoie, .345
Elmer Flick, .338

WINS BY A PITCHER

Steve Carlton, 241

Robin Roberts, 234

STOLEN BASES

Sherry Magee, 387

Jimmy Rollins, 326

WINS BY A MANAGER

Gene Mauch, 646

EARNED RUN AVERAGE

George McQuillan, 1.79

Lew Richie, 2.06

Glossary

All-Star a player who is named as one of the league's best and plays in the All-Star Game between the A.L. and the N.L.

Cy Young Award an award given to the top pitcher in each league

Gold Gloves awards given to the top fielder at each position in each league

Hall of Fame a building in Cooperstown, New York, where baseball's greatest players are honored

home plate a five-sided rubber pad where batters stand to swing, and where runners touch base to score runs

infield the area around and between the four bases of a baseball diamond

manager the person who is in charge of the team and chooses who will bat and pitch

mascots people in costume or animals that help fans cheer for their teams

Most Valuable Player (MVP) a yearly award given to the top player in each league

opponents teams or players that play against each other

outfield the large, grass area beyond the infield of a baseball diamond

Triple Crown leading a league in home runs, RBI, and batting average in the same season

World Series the Major League Baseball championship, played each year between the winners of the American and National Leagues

Find Out More

BOOKS

Buckley, James Jr. *Eyewitness Baseball*. New York: DK Publishing, 2010.

Savage, Jeff. *Ryan Howard*. Minneapolis: First Avenue Editions, 2008.

Stewart, Mark. *Philadelphia Phillies*. Chicago: Norwood House Press, 2008.

Teitelbaum, Michael. *Baseball*. Ann Arbor, MI: Cherry Lake Publishing, 2009.

WEB SITES

Visit our Web page for links about the Philadelphia Phillies and other pro baseball teams.

childsworld.com/links

Note to Parents, Teachers, and Librarians: We routinely verify our Web links to make sure they are safe, active sites—so encourage your readers to check them out!

Index

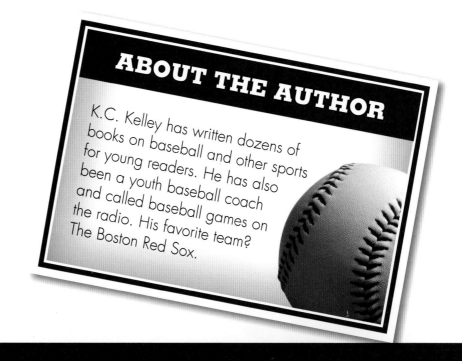

ABOUT THE AUTHOR

K.C. Kelley has written dozens of books on baseball and other sports for young readers. He has also been a youth baseball coach and called baseball games on the radio. His favorite team? The Boston Red Sox.